LIGHTNING
BOLT
BOOKS™

Purple Everywhere

Kristin Sterling

Lerner Publications Company

Minneapolis

Lerner Publications Company
A division of Lerner Publishing Group, Inc.
241 First Avenue North
Minneapolis, MN 55401 U.S.A.

Website address: www.lernerbooks.com

Library of Congress Cataloging-in-Publication Data

Sterling, Kristin.
    Purple everywhere / by Kristin Sterling.
        p.   cm. — (Lightning bolt books™— Colors everywhere)
    Includes index.
    ISBN 978-0-7613-5437-6 (lib. bdg. : alk. paper)
    1. Purple—Juvenile literature. 2. Colors—Juvenile literature. I. Title.
QC495.5.S7459 2011
535.6—dc22   2009044912

Manufactured in the United States of America
1 — CG — 7/15/10

Contents

A Purple World

Purple is magical. Purple is special. Purple is a color of unusual beauty.

Look around you.
Purple is everywhere!

These girls play on a purple slide.

Many of the foods you eat are purple. Eggplants are tasty purple vegetables.

Eggplants are deep purple on the outside and white on the inside.

Grapes are a healthful choice
for an after-school snack.

Patrick eats
a bunch.

Sometimes the sky turns
purple as the sun sets.
It is an awesome sight.

Pretty butterflies flit from flower to flower. Their wings look purple in the sunlight.

This butterfly is known as a small copper.

Purple things grow in gardens and fields. Irises are beautiful purple flowers.

Purple Japanese irises fill a field during the summer.

Lilac bushes bloom in the spring. You can make sweet-smelling bouquets of lilacs for your family or friends.

Purple can even be found in the sea.

Some sea stars are a bold purple color.

Purple crabs scoot across the shore. They are looking for a place to hide.

This purple crab crawls across a beach of broken shells.

Royal Purple

Purple is the color of royalty. For thousands of years, kings and queens wore purple clothes.

This painting shows a queen of Egypt wearing purple more than 2,200 years ago.

Only royal people could afford to wear purple. Long ago, purple dye was very expensive.

Cloth soaked in this dye will turn bright purple.

The saying Born to the Purple describes someone who is part of a royal family.

These people are members of the British Royal Family. Queen Elizabeth II is in front.

These
days,
anyone
can wear
purple!

Do you
have purple
clothes?

Shades of Purple

Purple is a mixture of red and blue. There are many shades of purple.

Some shades of purple are closer to blue, and some are closer to red. Some shades are light, and some are dark.

How many shades of purple can you find here?

Violet is a bluish shade of purple.

Rainbows appear when sunlight shines on tiny drops of water in the air.

You can see violet on the inner edge of a rainbow.

Plum is a reddish purple color.
Anna's mom is trying on
plum-colored lipstick.

Patty Loves Purple

Patty loves purple.
It is her favorite color!

Her room is decorated in shades of purple. She likes to have friends sleep over.

Patty feels like royalty in her purple bedroom.

Patty helps her parents in the garden. Her family grows purple cabbage.

Cabbage can have green, white, red, or purple leaves.

Sometimes Patty picks purple flowers. She makes bouquets to decorate the house.

Patty has a
purple guitar.
She plays in a
band with her
neighbors.

What is your favorite color?

Activity
Color Me a Carnation

Can flowers change colors? Try this fun experiment to find out!

What you need:
an adult to help you
a scissors
3 white carnations
3 flower vases or glasses
water
blue and red food coloring

What you do:

1. Have the adult use the scissors to trim the bottoms of the flower stems at an angle.

2. Fill the vases halfway with water.

3. In one vase, add several drops of blue food coloring. (Add enough so that the water has a blue tint.)

4. In another vase, add several drops of red food coloring.

5. In the last vase, add a few drops of both blue and red food coloring.

6. Put one carnation in each vase. Check on the flowers after one day has passed. What colors are the flowers? What happens after two days?

Glossary

bouquet: a bunch of flowers

dye: a liquid or powder used to change the color of something

expensive: having a high price

royalty: kings and queens and other members of a royal family

shade: the darkness or lightness of a color

unusual: rare, not seen often

Further Reading

Enchanted Learning: Purple/Violet
http://www.enchantedlearning.com/colors/purple.shtml

Henkes, Kevin. *Lilly's Purple Plastic Purse.* New York: Greenwillow Books, 1996.

Johnson, Crockett. *Harold and the Purple Crayon.* New York: HarperCollins, 2005.

Kessler, Leonard. *Mr. Pine's Purple House.* Cynthiana, KY: Purple House Press, 2005.

Ross, Kathy. *Kathy Ross Crafts Colors.* Minneapolis: Millbrook Press, 2003.

Stewart, Melissa. *Why Are Animals Purple?* Berkeley Heights, NJ: Enslow Elementary, 2009.

Index

Photo Acknowledgments

The images in this book are used with the permission of: © Grazvydas/Dreamstime.com, p. 1; © iStockphoto.com/Eileen Hart, p. 2; © Frederic Pacorel/Getty Images, p. 4; © Radius Images/CORBIS, p. 5; © iStockphoto.com/Joe_Potato, p. 6; © Kruchankova Maya/Shutterstock Images, p. 7; © Mike Brinson/Getty Images, p. 8; © Takashi Komiyama/Aflo Foto Agency/Photolibrary, p. 9; © iStockphoto.com/ArtEfficient, p. 10; © D. Sharon Pruitt Pink Sherbet Photography/Getty Images, p. 11; © Karoline Cullen/Shutterstock Images, p. 12; © Mike Shipman/Alamy, p. 13; © Leighton House Museum, Kensington & Chelsea, London, UK/The Bridgeman Art Library, p. 14; © age fotostock/SuperStock, p. 15; © Tim Graham/Tim Graham Photolibrary/Getty Images, p. 16; © Kevin Dodge/CORBIS, p. 17; © Todd Strand/Independent Picture Service, p. 18; © iStockphoto.com/Qweek, p. 19; © Jon Bower UK/Alamy, p. 20; © Gustavo Di Mario/Stone/Getty Images, p. 21; © Juice Images/CORBIS, p. 22, 25; © Richard Wheatley/Dorling Kindersley/Getty Images, p. 23; © Katrina Brown/Shutterstock Images, p. 24; © Keith Publicover/Shutterstock Images, p. 26; © iStockphoto.com/ArtisticCaptures, p. 27; © iStockphoto.com/Ljupco, p. 28 (pitcher); © iStockphoto.com/John A Meents, p. 28 (food coloring); © iStockphoto.com/TerrainScan, p. 28 (vase); © www.images.paulsampson.com, p. 28 (flower); © iStockphoto.com/Scott Hogge, p. 28 (scissors); © iStockphoto.com/Sanne Berg, p. 30; © Tal Silverman/TS Photography/Getty Images, p. 31.

Front cover: © David Hall/The Image Works (fish); © J2Odb/Dreamstime.com (flower); © iStockphoto.com/alle12 (grapes); © iStockphoto.com/Bradley Mason (rainboots); © iStockphoto.com/Lisa Thornberg (butterfly); © Nick Laham/Getty Images (Vikings football player).